JEEP OFF-ROAD

First published in 2007 by Motorbooks, an imprint of MBI Publishing Company LLC, Galtier Plaza, Suite 200, 380 Jackson Street, St. Paul, MN 55101 USA

Motorbooks titles are also available at discounts in bulk quantity for industrial or sales-promotional use. For details write to Special Sales Manager at MBI Publishing Company, Galtier Plaza, Suite 200, 380 Jackson Street, St. Paul, MN 55101 USA.

To find out more about our books, join us online at www.motorbooks.com.

ISBN-13: 978-0-7603-2994-8
ISBN-10: 0-7603-2994-X

Editor: Peter Schletty
Designer: Michael Cawcutt

Printed in China

About the author: Formerly a staff editor at *Four Wheeler*, *Off-Road* and *4x4 Power* magazines, Tom Morr has contributed articles to many off-road enthusiast and trade publications worldwide. He lives in Southern California.

About the photographer: Ken Brubaker's work has appeared in a variety of magazines, including *Four Wheeler*, *4 Wheel & Off-Road*, *Off-Road*, *4 Wheel Drive & Sport Utility*, *Fullsize 4x4*, and many others. He lives in Northern Illinois with his wife and three children.

On the cover: Events like the Ramsey National Off-Road Challenge require drivers to think on the fly while traversing brutal obstacles.

On the frontispiece: Although this Jeep looks pristine, here it's conquering the trails at the Total Off-Road Rally near Dresser, Wisconsin.

On the title pages: Too fast for fender flares. Thrust and inertia can cause broken parts to fly. Mud always seems to stick, though.

On the back cover: *Left:* Built on the same platform as the WK Grand Cherokee, the Commander is two inches longer and has a larger body to accommodate seven passengers comfortably. *Middle:* A custom spare carrier and can holder attends to business in the rear of this 1970 Commando. *Right:* Once the decision is made to stretch a CJ-3A, why not go all out and hack the hood to make way for a blown big block?

Library of Congress Cataloging-in-Publication Data
Morr, Tom, 1963–
 Jeep off-road / text by Tom Morr ; photography by Ken Brubaker.
p. cm.
 Includes bibliographical references.
 ISBN-13: 978-0-7603-2994-8 (softbound)
 ISBN-10: 0-7603-2994-X (softbound)
 1. Jeep automobile—History. I. Brubaker, Ken, 1963– II. Title.
TL215.J44M67 2007
796.7—dc22
                              2007002666

Contents

Introduction

Acknowledgments

Several experts had their hands in this text, either directly or otherwise. Granville King, the godfather of off-road writing, is the spiritual inspiration for much of our information. His *Jeep Bible* (www.jeepbible.com), first published in 1985 and since revised and updated by Willie Worthy, set the standard for informative yet entertainingly accessible books about Jeeps. An example of King's pull-no-punches dispatches from Baja is included here.

Other current and former colleagues who helped me separate Jeep fact from fiction over the years include the aforementioned Worthy, tech guru extraordinaire, and Jim Allen, whose thoroughly researched books are valuable to everyone who's passionate about Jeeps and the history of four-wheel-drive vehicles. Trent "As Seen on TV" McGee is always generous with his Gen Y perspective on Jeeps. Other industry legends who've been gracious with their time and knowledge over the past 20-some-odd years include Brian Chuchua, Mark Smith, Don Adams (the racer turned buffalo rancher, not Maxwell Smart), Bret Lovett, Jason Bunch, Oly and Kate Olson, the late Lloyd Novak, and Mike Schwellinger.

DaimlerChrysler PR also contributed to this cause. Gratitude goes to Nick Cappa and Christina Biache, who tracked down the recent Jeep sales numbers included here.

The "flat-fender nazis" (a term of pure endearment) deserve their own paragraph of kudos. Charter member Jimmy Nylund was enamored enough with his CJ-3A to bring it, $20 in kronor, and a change of clothes from Sweden to America. Another flat-fender aficionado, Ned "Killer Bee" Bacon is an automotive historian par excellence disguised by a flannel shirt.

Ninety-weight thanks go to Rick Péwé. I've never met anyone else who tastes your Jeep's fluids before introducing himself. Péwé has fixed my Jeep and enhanced my magazine articles many times. He allowed himself to be begged into QC duties for this book, on top of his more-than-fulltime duties at *4-Wheel & Off-Road* and his ongo-

The word *Jeep* was invented by cartoonist Elzie Crisler (E. C.) Segar in the comic strip that became known as "Popeye." Allegedly, Segar checked English and foreign dictionaries to ensure that the word wasn't already in use.

ing personal crusade to ensure that no orphaned Jeep goes unadopted.

Nearly last but definitely not least, Peter Schletty at MBI Publishing managed/edited this project. His patience and willingness to turn a deaf ear to "only 50 more custom-Jeep-in-Moab captions to go" was appreciated. Finally, the Brubaker and Morr families deserve a big dinner out. Becky, Rachel, Dan and Dave Brubaker, and Lori Morr were inhumanly patient (Garrett Morr doesn't know that virtue yet) while Ken and I holed up with Jeep stuff for much longer than expected. Somehow, time flies when dealing with Jeeps because it doesn't seem like work.

Jeep Gallery

The Jeep is greater than the sum of its parts. Its DNA makes the Jeep a genetic freak in the automotive world. Can you name one other brand that's outlived four parent companies? The Jeep pulse still beats after more than 65 years, unlike former progenitors Willys, Kaiser, AMC, AMC/Renault, and Chrysler (counting the Teutonic DaimlerChrysler as a different entity from the AMC-absorbing, all-American Iacocca/Lutz/Eaton company).

Jeep scholars know that the original military Jeep was actually conceived by Bantam. However, the government awarded its 1/4-ton 4x4 reconnaissance vehicle contract to Willys-Overland Motors, later enlisting Ford to help meet increased production demands. This gives Jeep perhaps the bushiest-branched family tree in all of autodom: Bantam, Willys, Ford, Kaiser, AMC/Renault, Chrysler, and DaimlerChrysler.

Until recently, the Jeep's history was, well, documented. It's now well documented, thanks to researchers and writers such as Jim Allen who've identified and resolved many of the discrepancies between "official" records and firsthand accounts by former Toledo-based Willys-Overland employees and military veterans.

Military History

To make a long story somewhat shorter, the Jeep's lineage dates back to at least World War I. General "Black Jack" Pershing shipped some Jeffrey "Quad" 4x4 trucks to France, having previously used these vehicles to search for Pancho Villa in Mexico. The army then embraced the effectiveness of an off-pavement vehicle that ran on tires, not tracks. By the 1930s, Marmon-Harrington 4x4-converted Ford trucks that sold the army on the value of four-wheel drive.

Another army concern was the size of the moving target. The 1937–1939 Howie-Wiley "Belly Flopper" went overboard in this respect. Literally a low-profile vehicle, the Belly Flopper got its nickname from the soldiers' riding position: prone on a flat deck between a fore-mounted machine gun and an engine at the rear.

After World War II broke out, the army released specs for its proposed 1/4-ton 4x4 reconnaissance vehicle: 80-inch wheelbase, 47-inch track width, 600-pound payload, overall weight of 1,300 pounds, and 49 days to deliver a prototype. Only three of the then-135 American car companies bid on the project: Bantam, Ford, and Willys-Overland.

The first test vehicle, built by Bantam, was delivered to the army proving ground at Camp Holabird, Maryland, on September 23, 1940. More than 2,600 Bantam Reconnaissance Cars (BRC-40s) were subsequently built in 1941, after which the company quit the automobile business. Willys' Quad model won the military contract, primarily due to its impressive "Go Devil" L-head four-cylinder engine. Ford's Pygmy had the best overall design, and many of its specs were integrated into the Willys MB—the vehicle that would launch the Jeep mystique worldwide.

The Universal Word

Linguists claim that *okay* is the word that's most known worldwide. Fifty years ago, *Jeep* was the universal word. At the end of World War II and throughout the Korean and Vietnam conflicts, people in all corners of the earth became familiar with the Jeep Universal, the short-wheelbase vehicle that General George C. Marshall called "America's greatest contribution to modern warfare." That's quite a compliment coming from a man who was army chief of staff during the Manhattan Project and was influential in initiating atomic warfare.

Beloved World War II correspondent Ernie Pyle lavished similar praise on the Jeep before being killed in combat in 1945: "The Jeep—Good Lord, I don't think we could continue the war without it! It does anything. It goes anywhere. It's faithful as a dog, strong as a mule, and agile as a goat."

The origin of the Jeep name for the 1/4-ton four-wheel-drive military general-purpose reconnaissance vehicle used to be debated. A popular myth had World War II GIs slurring GP—an acronym for "general purpose" that was apparently applied to everything from toothpaste to underwear—to create Jeep. Another left-field explanation had Jeep coming from the

Bombastic engine nicknames are part of the Jeep charm. The original 60-horsepower "Go Devil," surplus Buick-designed "Dauntless" V-6, and numerous other powerplant monikers actually make the modern Hemi sound somewhat sedate.

GPW, Ford's version of the Willys MB.

The actual word undoubtedly came from a character in the popular "Thimble Theater, Starring Popeye" comic strip. Cartoonist E. C. Segar introduced Eugene the Jeep on March 16, 1936. Eugene's supernatural powers included teleportation, the ability to go anywhere anytime. (Many Jeep clubs use Eugene as their mascot. Mile-Hi Jeep Club HoboJeepers have several of the strips featuring Eugene on their website: http://members.tripod.com/HoboJeepers)

Eugene's go-anywhere ability resulted in various industrial and four-wheel-drive vehicles receiving the nickname "Jeep" in the late 1930s. National Guardsmen reportedly referred to a Minneapolis-Moline 4x4 tractor conversion as a Jeep at a 1940 testing session in Camp Ripley, Minnesota. The 1940–1941 1/2-ton Dodge Command Reconnaissance truck was also called a Jeep while the 1/4-ton version was the Peep; 3/4-ton Command Cars were Beeps (for "big Jeeps").

By 1942, the name applied only to the 1/4-ton bobtail 4x4 vehicle. Esteemed automotive writer Granville King, who served in the army during World War II and claimed to be in a foxhole a couple hundred yards from Ernie Pyle when sniper fire killed the war correspondent, spelled out the name debate in his book *The Jeep Bible*:

In early 1941, we had all those crazy Pygmys, BRCs, and Quads rushing about the country, but none were called "Jeep" at the time. The army had some 1/2-ton Dodge Command Recon Trucks they called "Jeeps," it is

A letter from Granville King, the godfather of the Jeep cult, exemplifies the passion for these vehicles and the places they take us.

said. And so old-time sergeants called the new breed "Peeps." Red Hausmann, test driver for Willys, always called his rig a Jeep because he said it "shouldn't be mixed up with those funny Bugs, Midgets, BRCs, and such at Camp Holabird."

Although King privately admitted to occasionally massaging the facts for dramatic effect in his writings, he was always adamant about the origin of the name *Jeep* in personal correspondence and conversation, even when conventional wisdom still subscribed to the GP explanation.

TJ Wranglers

TJ Wranglers

For purists, the TJ brought back the "True Jeep." Possibly provoked by the "Real Jeeps Don't Have Square Headlights" T-shirts and bumper stickers that spawned from the YJ Wrangler, Chrysler engineers retained about 80 percent of the first-generation Wrangler (the tailgates are even identical). They then added $260 million worth of changes—including 7-inch round headlights—to dress up the TJ. Coil springs at each corner initially raised eyebrows, but one test drive convinced even the dustiest, crustiest, grizzliest old-timer that this was the best production bobtail street-legal off-roader ever built.

Some changes, such as dual airbags, were government mandated while others where inspired by globalization—for example, a modular dash allowed left- and right-hand-drive models to be produced on the same assembly line. Amenities such as softer seats and cupholders were cribbed from the ZJ Grand Cherokee.

Never mind the modern air conditioning and improved aerodynamics and materials that allowed ragtop conversations at highway speeds. The coil springs actually absorbed the buckboard ride inherent in short-wheelbase vehicles at higher speeds. Off-road, they offered greater travel and articulation than the time-honored leaf packs they replaced.

Actually, the TJ's coils were more evolutionary than revolutionary: The factory-dubbed Quadra Coil system was stolen from the ZJ Grand Cherokee. Hardcore rock crawlers began experimenting with coil-over suspensions in the early 1990s to achieve axle droop far in excess of what was possible with leafs. Shortly before the TJ was unveiled, Black Diamond (then a division of Warn Industries, now under Superlift ownership) introduced the XCL kit to convert YJs and CJs to four-corner coils. Regardless of whether hardcore Jeep enthusiasts or the aftermarket influenced Chrysler's engineers, the Quadra Coil TJ became the best-suspended Jeep Universal yet.

Good Stuff

Powerwise, true enthusiasts aren't moved by four-bangers, and even the stock 4.0L six-cylinder engines are routinely livened up with freer-breathing aftermarket intakes and exhausts, Unichip tuning, Edge Trail Jammer systems (intake, big-bore throttle body, and computer module), Golen 4.6L stroker kits, Avenger or Kenne-Bell superchargers, or countless other power-makers. For others, anything less than eight cylinders won't cut it. These people become well acquainted with Advance Adapters, Novak Enterprises, and other companies that specialize in Jeep powertrain swaps.

The factory gearboxes that back the six-bangers all have good reputations for durability. Of the five-speeds, the AX-15 (1997–1999) and NV3550 are virtually interchangeable; the latter is heavier-duty but noisier. The NSG370 six-speed (2005–2006) is even more highly evolved, with its 4.46:1 first gear compared to the AX-15's 3.83:1 first. Unfortunately, an integral bell housing prevents the six-speed from being a straightforward swap into Jeeps that don't have the 4.0L six or 2.4L four-banger.

The early-run transfer case (NP231) and axles (Dana 30 front, Dana 35C rear) were basically carryovers from the YJ. The main difference was that the front axle lacked a disconnect mechanism. Midway into the first year of production, the venerable Dana 44 rear axle became an option. This foreshadowed good things ahead.

Rubicon to the Rescue

In 2003, the Rubicon model offered off-road enthusiasts aftermarket-inspired powertrain equipment backed by a factory warranty. Most notable were 4.10-geared Dana 44 front and rear axles, both with driver-selectable Tru-Lok lockers. The other marquee feature was the NV241OR Rock-Trac transfer case with its 4:1 low-range gearing. Jeepers only had to install a lift kit and larger tires to be truly trail-ready.

Unlimited Wrangler potential was incited by the 103.4-inch wheelbase Unlimited model, introduced in 2005. Channeling the classic CJ-8/Scrambler, the Unlimited offered 13 additional linear inches for cargo and slightly more legroom for back-seat passengers.

If the CJ-8 is the grandfather, then the Unlimited TJ is daddy to the 2007 four-door JK Wrangler, which was released as this book went to press. A book devoted to the JK was undoubtedly already in the works before the vehicle went on sale.

Clifton Slay of Poison Spyder Customs calls his TJ *Atrax Robustus* "the world's deadliest spider." The concept was bolt-on performance, demonstrated by a Superlift 6-inch Rockrunner lift, Detroit Locker traction devices, and Mastercraft suspension seats.

2000 TJ
Owner: Clifton Slay, Sheridan, Colorado
Engine: 4.0L I-6
Transmission: TF999 auto
Axles: D30 front, Detroit Truetrac; D44 rear, Detroit Electrac; 4.56 gears
Tires: 35x12.50-17 Mickey Thompson Baja Radial Claws
Wheels: 17x9 Mickey Thompson Classic IIs
Suspension: Superlift 6-inch Rockrunner kit
Accessories: AEV Heat Reduction Hood, paint by Poor Boy Kustoms (Loveland, Colorado)

Poison Spyder Customs armor includes the Stinger front bumper, steering box skid plate, Rock Ring diff protectors, Tube Fenders, Trail Corners, and Rocker Knockers.

The full Poison Spyder Customs roll cage is one of the few non-bolt-ons—it's a production kit but requires welding. Rolling stock is 35-inch Baja Claws that secure to 17x9 MT Classic II wheels with OMF bead locks.

Jerry Therrien's 1998 TJ has been from Florida to Moab. Retro flat fenders make extra room for a Rubicon Express 4.5-inch lift kit and 35-inch BFG Mud-Terrains.

1998 TJ
Owner: Jerry Therrien, Tarpon Springs, Florida
Engine: 4.0L I-6, Turbo City throttle body and intake, K&N filter, Borla header
Transmission: TF999 auto
Transfer Case: Atlas II
Axles: D30 front, ARB Air Locker; D44 rear, ARB Air Locker; 4.56 gears
Suspension: Rubicon Express 4.5-inch kit, Doetsch Tech shocks
Tires: 35x12.50-15 MFG Mud-Terrains
Wheels: 15x10 bead locks
Accessories: Warn 9,000-pound winch, Rock Krawler bumpers, Rusty's tie rods

The stalwart 4.0 received some extra life from a Turbo City throttle body and cold-air intake, a K&N filter, and a Borla header that leads to a Gibson cat-back exhaust.

Red Gator Liner paint protects the interior. Therrien uses all available space for storage, and the rear Rock Krawler bumper doubles as a compressed-air storage tank.

Therrien's interior is strictly business. It's protected by a custom six-point roll cage installed by Innovative Chassis of Ocala, Florida. Custom rear trunks add secure storage.

Scott Allen's Solar Yellow TJ is accessorized with a Warn HS9500i winch, Hella auxiliary lights, and Tomken Rock Sliders.

2000 TJ
Owner: Scott Allen, Ocala, Florida
Engine: Dakota 4.7L V-8, custom exhaust, Flowmaster mufflers
Transmission: NV4500
Transfer Case: Atlas II
Axles: High-pinion D60s, Detroit Lockers, Strange shafts, 5.13 gears
Suspension: Rubicon Express 8-inch Long Arm kit, Doetsch Tech shocks
Tires: 38.5x16-15 MT Baja Claws
Wheels: 15x10 Center Line Thrusters
Accessories: Warn winch, Hella lights, Currie rear bumper/tire rack, Tomken Rocker Skids

A Dakota donated its 4.7L Hemi. Custom wiring and exhaust were necessary, as was modifying a Lakewood bell housing to accommodate the NV4500 gearbox.

Big skins required 8 inches of lift, a Rubicon Express Long Arm kit, in this case. Steering linkage is custom, as is the high-pinion Dana 60 rig.

A Currie rear bumper/spare carrier accommodates a full-size fifth piece of rolling stock. The custom Dana 60 rear end is also visible.

Jesse Meyer bought his TJ new, then dismantled it in his shop, Mudder Truckers. The frame was lengthened 20 inches.

2000 TJ
Owner: Jesse Meyer, Milford, Ohio
Engine: 4.0L I-6, K&N filter, Purple Meanie mufflers
Transmission: TF999 auto, B&M cooler
Transfer Case: Atlas II
Axles: Ford D60 front; Chevy 14-bolt rear; Detroit Lockers, 4.56 gears
Suspension: Custom four-link, 8-inch lift, RaceRunner and Skyjacker shocks
Tires: 39.5x15-15 Super Swampers
Wheels: 15x10 Eaton bead locks
Accessories: TSM disc brakes, Warn 9500 winch, TeraFlex skid plate

Left: A basically stock straight-six sits under the modified hood. A RaceRunner coil-over shock is in the foreground, and part of the AGR steering is visible.

Top: A custom four-link setup yields eight inches of Super-Swamper-clearing lift. The custom 'cage attaches to the frame.

Meyer is a firm believer in lightness. He likes the doorless effect, and interior mods are limited to a Tuffy console, a B&M trans-temp gauge, and RCI harnesses.

Dr. Ray Woo is an orthopedic surgeon who relaxes with the Ocala Jeep Club. An ARB front bumper holds Hella and IPF lights; the Bullet-proof rear bumper incorporates a Jamboree rack.

1998 TJ
Owner: Ray Woo, Gainesville, Florida
Engine: 4.0L I-6, Turbo City intake, K&N filter, Borla exhaust
Transmission: TF999 auto, B&M cooler
Transfer Case: NP231, JB SYE
Axles: D30 front, EZ Locker; D44 rear, Detroit SofLocker, 4.56 gears
Suspension: TeraFlex 4-inch lift, Air Lift bags, Rancho RS9000 shocks; 1-inch body lift
Tires: 35-inch BFG AT KOs
Wheels: 15x10 American Racing Bajas
Accessories: Ramsey Pro Plus 9000 winch, Terra & Tomken skid plates, Hella and IPF lights

Woo's engine breathes better with a Turbo City intake and K&N filter. Other aftermarket additions include an Optima battery.

Interior upgrades include a Tuffy console, an Eagle GPS, a QuickAir compressor, a mega-watt stereo, and a 'cage-mounted camcorder.

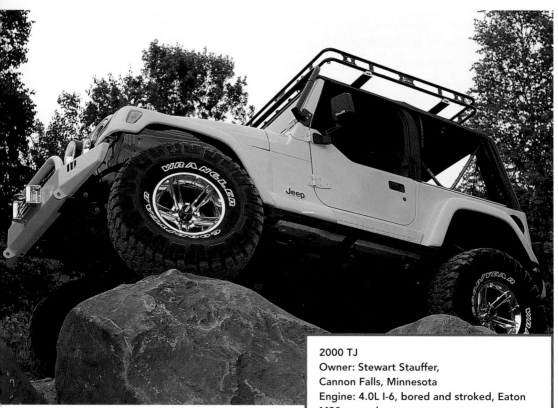

Burnsville Off-Road in Minnesota built Stewart Stauffer's TJ with plenty of TeraFlex components, including a 4-inch lift, skid plates, 4:1 T-case gears, and slip-yoke eliminator.

2000 TJ
Owner: Stewart Stauffer,
Cannon Falls, Minnesota
Engine: 4.0L I-6, bored and stroked, Eaton M90 supercharger
Transmission: NV4500 five-speed
Transfer Case: NP231, TeraFlex 4:1 kit and SYE
Axles: Dynatrac high-pinion D44 front, ARB Air Locker; Dynatrac high-pinion D60 rear, ARB Air Locker, 4.56 gears
Suspension: TeraFlex 4-inch lift, Trail Master shocks
Tires: 35x12.50-15 Wrangler MT/Rs
Wheels: 15x8 MKWs
Accessories: M.O.R.E. front bumper, Burnsville Off-Road rear bumper and rock rails, Warn HS9500 winch, TeraFlex skid plates, IPF lights, functional custom hood scoop, chrome-moly steering linkage, KargoMaster roof rack, Clarion voice-activated stereo system, heated and ventilated Recaro seats

Left: A Mountain Off-Road Enterprises front bumper was color matched to the TJ. Although the Jeep looks pristine, here it's conquering the trails at the Total Off-Road Rally near Dresser, Wisconsin.

Top: Dan McKeag at Burnsville Off-Road built the stock 4.0L with a stroker kit and an Eaton supercharger. The engine puts out 367 horsepower under 11 pounds of boost.

IPF auxiliary lights illuminate the way after dark and in inclement weather. A Warn winch is on standby in case of a stuck.

Sandstone and snow: This TJ is prepped for Moab's Easter Jeep Safari with wilderness-style storage racks. The view is tough to beat.

TJ Specifications

Wheelbase: 93.4 inches
Length: 151.8 inches
Height: 66.7 inches
Width: 68.9 inches
Curb Weight: 3,229 pounds

X-trim TJs rolled off the line with a 190-horsepower 4.0L and NV3550 five-speed. This example is rock-ready on Yokohama Geolander A/Ts with rock-crawler-style rims. It also has a Raingler cargo net system and Light Force driving lights on the aftermarket front bumper.

Like soft drink cans, aluminum bodies wrinkle. However, they don't rust and are a more affordable alternative to aftermarket fiberglass Jeep tubs, fenders, and hoods.

Moab's slickrock terrain is ironically named since it actually provides decent traction. Otherwise, this Unlimited TJ would be precariously close to imminent doom.

If this TJ's owner were a professional wrestler, his name might possibly be Mr. Flexy. This Jeep is just one example of the custom 4x4s that attend the Vegas Valley 4 Wheelers' Hump N Bump event every November.

1997 Base TJ MSRPs	
Wrangler SE:	$13,495
Wrangler Sport:	$17,192
Wrangler Sahara:	$19,263

More Moab action: This TJ is equipped with popular ways to increase bite on the rocks. These include Goodyear Wrangler MT/R tires, a Rock Krawler suspension system, and Currie Enterprises Antirock sway bars.

Off the assembly line, the TJ is the most trail-capable Jeep to date. Owners can simply add a suspension lift with bigger tires for increased ground clearance and "gription."

Rubicon trim adds even more aftermarket-inspired capability to the stock TJ, including 4:1 low-range gearing and selectable differential lockers. Poison Spyder outfitted this one with their company's armor in addition to other Moab-ready items.

Top: Jeep Jamboree events lure enthusiasts to some of the country's most scenic backcountry areas, many of which are on private property.

Inset: Daily driver TJs are competition-ready with a few improvements. Visible here are aftermarket tires, wheels, a lift, a winch, and a snorkel.

1997 Performance
2.5L I-4: 120 horsepower @ 5,400 rpm, 140 lb-ft @ 3,500 rpm
4.0L I-6: 181 horsepower @ 4,600 rpm, 222 lb-ft @ 2,800 rpm

1999 Performance
4.0L I-6: 190 horsepower @ 4,600 rpm, 235 lb-ft @ 3,200 rpm

2003 Performance
2.4L I-4: 147 horsepower @ 5,200 rpm, 165 lb-ft @ 4,000 rpm

Top: This New Mexico-based Rubicon lives up to its personalized license plate. The Las Cruces area is well-known for its challenging terrain.

Inset: Boat detailer Eric Altom of Ketchum, Oklahoma, is usually up for anything in his "Bloody Cow" stretch-wheelbase TJ. He placed well here in the 2001 Ramsey National Off-Road Challenge.

This TJ from Maximum Offroad in Las Vegas greets the sun at the Nevada Hump N Bump event. Modifications include a TeraFlex lift, IPF lights, and a Ramsey winch.

Popular TJ Factory Paint Colors

Black
Bright Jade Satin Glow
Flame Red
Emerald Green
Moss Green
Lapis Blue
Deep Amethyst
Chili Pepper Red Pearlcoat
Stone White
Gunmetal Pearlcoat
Forest Green Pearlcoat
Desert Sand Pearlcoat
Intense Blue Pearlcoat
Medium Fern Green Pearlcoat
Solar Yellow
Patriot Blue Pearlcoat
Silverstone Metallic
Inca Gold Pearlcoat

Sportsman classes offer Average Joes the chance to run in organized rock-crawling competitions. Body damage is a common price of success.

The late, great, Safari Triathlon series inspired plenty of mechanical carnage. Competitors had to ready themselves and their vehicles for day and night challenges.

Discovered by mud runners in full-sized 4x4s, Super Swamper Bogger tires are popular with hardcore TJ owners who like to attack gumbo goo as well as granite.

TJ Trim Packages	
1997:	SE
1997:	Sport
1997:	Sahara
2002:	X
2003:	Rubicon
2005:	Unlimited

TJs look totally at home in Florida's Ocala National Forest during an Ocala Jeep Club Swamp Run.

Many owners bought their TJs for commuting through inclement weather, only to discover the fun of playing in the snow.

YJ WRANGLERS

YJ Wranglers

The *60 Minutes* Jeep rollover segment, which aired on December 21, 1980, crafted the CJ's coffin. AMC engineers soon began drafting a lower-center-of-gravity successor: the pavement-biased YJ Wrangler with more carlike creature comforts, which hit the market in mid-1986 as a 1987 model.

It was quickly dubbed the "Yuppie Jeep" by CJ cultists. Rectangular headlights were particularly offensive to traditionalists. A further insult was the 1991 Renegade package and its bulbous fiberglass fenders. This automotive fashion felony was the butt of many jokes, possibly one-upped only by the Chevy Avalanche's hideous gray body cladding. (The Renegade option mercifully disappeared for 1994.)

The Wrangler's geartrain didn't earn many fans off-road. The vehicle was launched with a five-speed Peugeot transmission—somewhat curious since AMC's corporate French bedfellow at the time was Renault. In 1987 models, additional gear reduction came from an NP207 transfer case, which had a 2.61 low-range. It was quickly orphaned, replaced by the 2.72 low-ranged NP231 for the 1988 model year.

On a positive note, the YJ's frame was actually stouter than the CJ's. Further, the Wrangler received the 180-horsepower AMC 4.0L "Power Tech Six" in 1991, replacing the ubiquitous and torquey 258-ci/4.2L straight six.

Reviving Wranglers

Hardcore off-roaders consider YJs the adopted red-headed bastard stepchildren of the Jeep Universal family. Owners who'd rather spend more time driving off-road than turning wrenches are bang-per-buck better off starting with a used TJ or an already-customized CJ.

Fortunately, used YJs are some of the most affordable Jeep customizing platforms. Because Wranglers are popular high-school graduation presents, many unabused "sorority girl" YJs are on the used market. Competent mechanics who know their ways around junkyards can often affordably create tremendously trail-worthy YJs.

Beginning up front, upgrade options are plentiful. The front axle's vacuum-actuated 4WD lock-in system is its Achilles' heel. The easiest fix is to replace the vacuum line with a pull-cable system such as the Posi-Lok. More expensive is a manual-hub conversion kit such as the one from Warn, which includes hardened axle shafts. In the rear, the Dana 35C's C-clip axle-retention setup is suspect when combined with oversized tires. Aftermarket C-clip eliminator kits are one solution.

Owners who want to run larger than 33-inch tires will likely want to regear the ring-and-pinions to 4.10 or 4.56. Diff discussions lead to aftermarket traction devices, and custom-assembled axles often become an option, particularly if disc brakes are on the wish list. A custom-cut Dana 44 is popular for the front. In the rear, the Ford 8.8 from an Explorer/Ranger is virtually a bolt-in (once the spring pads are welded on) and includes disc brakes. The Dana 44 is another popular rear swap, and the huge-tire hardcore people eventually settle on a custom Dana 60 in the rear and possibly a second one up front.

The above-mentioned Peugeot BA 10/5 five-speed manual transmission is basically a loser. The easiest swap is a 1989–1994 Aisin-Warner AX-15; heavier-duty NV3500 and NV4500 implants are also popular due to lower first gears and overall strength.

The NP231 T-case's inherently leaky tailshaft can be fixed with an aftermarket slip-yoke eliminator kit. This also accommodates a longer rear driveshaft. Available 4:1 gear kits make the NP231 a keeper for most; the hardcore faction prefers the stout yet pricey Atlas and Orion aftermarket T-cases.

Overall, vocal-minority YJ owners are actually proud of the efforts they've undertaken to make their "Yuppies" into respectable off-road machines. Others grow tired of the razzing and adapt a TJ grille and its round headlights.

A 20-year CJ-2A owner, Dave Buczynski is a Jeep purist. He bought a YJ Renegade from the classifieds and attempted to convert a "city Jeep" into a respectable off-road machine.

1993 Wrangler Renegade
Owner: Dave Buczynski, Cloquet, Minnesota
Engine: 4.0L I-6
Transmission: TF 999 auto, B&M SuperCooler
Transfer Case: NP231, Currie SYE, TeraLow 4:1 kit
Axles: D30 front, Detroit TrueTrac; D44 rear, Detroit Locker; 4.56 gears
Suspension: BDS 3.5-inch kit, 1.5-inch extended shackles, Trailmaster SSV shocks; 2-inch TeraFlex body lift
Tires: 35x12.50-15 Super Swamper Boggers
Wheels: 15x10 MRT bead locks
Accessories: Warn XD9000i winch, Midwest 4WD rear bumper/tire carrier, Bosch driving lights, flames by Burnsville Off-Road

Boggers on MRT bead locks are about as serious as it gets. Buczynski combined a BDS lift kit with other components to make clearance.

Gross 'glass served as a canvas for painter Dan McKeag. The flames are subtle during the day and come to life as the sun lowers in the sky.

There's nothing yuppie about Ernie "Big E" Prevedel's YJ. Prowler Orange paint by Johnny Bullion, a pirated powertrain from Chevy, and I-H 4x4s make it unique.

1998 Wrangler
Owner: Ernie "Big E" Prevedel, Lady Lake, Florida
Engine: Chevy 400-ci V-8, Holley Pro-Jection EFI, Weiand intake, DynoMax headers
Transmission: TH400, B&M converter and shift kit
Transfer Case: Dana 300
Axles: D44 front, Trac-Lok; D60 rear, Detroit Locker; 4.56 gears
Suspension: Rubicon Express 4-inch kit, Revolver shackles, Skyjacker shocks
Tires: 35x12.50-15 Pro Comp Mud-Terrains
Wheels: 15x10 Pro Comp Rock Crawlers
Accessories: Warn 8000i winch, Hella lights

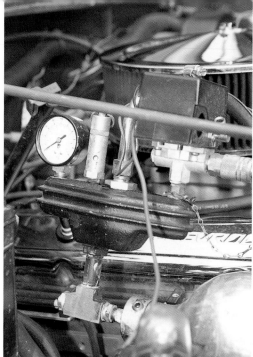

TeraFlex Revolver shackles allow added articulation from the Rubicon Express springs. Big E designed and fabricated the bumpers himself.

A custom onboard air system uses a Delco AC compressor. The 375-horsepower Chevy 400 V-8 has KB pistons, a Comp cam, a Mallory ignition, and Holley EFI.

The interior is good to go, thanks to a custom cage, a Garmin GPS, a Cobra CB, Bestop Super Seats, and a Tuffy console.

Fred Perry of Clemson 4 Wheel Center in South Carolina built his YJ to conquer trails across the country, including mining roads in Colorado's San Juan Mountains during a Telluride Rotary Club 4x4 event.

Chevy small-block power transforms this Wrangler into a Strangler. Visible good stuff includes tunable SuperTrapp mufflers and full-floating rear axle shafts.

YJ Specifications
Wheelbase: 93.4 inches
Length: 152 inches
Height: 68.9 inches
Width: 66 inches
Curb Weights: 2,869 to 3,023 pounds

Top: This Volunteer State YJ blasts off. Its astronaut likely lost more than the winch cover upon reentry to earth.

Inset: Even ultra-aggressive Super Swamper Boggers couldn't claw through deep New Hampshire powder here. Fortunately, this Wrangler has a winch.

1987 Base MSRPs
Wrangler S: $8,795
Wrangler Sport: $10,620
Wrangler Laredo: $12,205

Top: Add style points for one tire deep in a rut and one way up in the air. Subtract points due to driver Hasselhoffing out the cockpit.

Inset: Jeep Jamborees attract owners of all ilks and a range of rigs. This normally easygoing couple—based on the airbrushed slogan—gets a bit exuberant in their personalized YJ.

Top: Nicknamed "Trail Doggy," this Iowa-bred Wrangler rides the rut, giving its driver pure side-hill bliss.

Inset: BFG Mud-Terrains spray snow during an Eastern 4 Wheelers Winter Club Run in New Hampshire. The Wrangler was customized by Trail-Smith 4x4 in Connecticut.

Top: Superlift's "Woods Ready" YJ competed in ProROCK events. Trent "As Seen on TV" McGee spotted Bret Lovett into a rollover shortly after this shot was snapped.

Inset: Competitive rock crawling is a great way to bang your metal in front of a crowd. This coil-converted YJ features a rock-sculpted tub.

1987 Performance
2.5L I-4: 117 horsepower @ 5,000 rpm, 135 lb-ft @ 3,500 rpm
4.2L I-6: 112 horsepower @ 4,600 rpm, 210 lb-ft @ 2,000 rpm

1991 Performance
2.5L I-4: 123 horsepower @ 5,250 rpm, 139 ft-lb @ 3,000 rpm
4.0L I-6: 180 horsepower @ 4,750 rpm, 220 lb-ft @ 4,000 rpm

1993 Performance
2.5L I-4: 130 horsepower @ 5,250 rpm, 149 ft-lb @ 3,000 rpm
4.0L H.O. I-6: 190 horsepower @ 4,750 rpm, 225 lb-ft @ 4,000 rpm

Top: In 1994, Black Diamond's XCL coil-conversion kit sparked interest in longer-travel suspensions for CJs and YJs. Chrysler jumped on the bandwagon with the TJ Wrangler in 1997.

Inset: Based in Billings, Missouri, John Lloyd's extended-wheelbase "Scrangler" YJ is a fixture at competitive events and off-road parks.

Top: John Lloyd gets his Scrangler dirty at a Ramsey Winch Off-Road Challenge event. At least his stainless-steel roll cage won't rust.

Inset: Carnivorous photographer goes through protein withdrawal during a now-defunct Rosser Rendezvous event.

Special Trim Packages
1987: Laredo
1987: S
1988: Sahara
1989: Islander
1991: Renegade
1993: Sport

Top: Enthusiasts admire the scenery while this Wrangler's owner searches the hill for his AAA card.

Inset: Here's how Idaho Jeep owners break the ice. This spotter apparently drew the short straw while the driver languishes behind the heat vents.

Top: The "Anomaly" YJ finds itself between the proverbial rock and a hard place during the Vegas Valley 4 Wheelers' annual Hump N Bump event.

Inset: Superlift's Bret Lovett gets crossed up with those confusing "right/correct/military right" spotting instructions. Jeep windshield frames are notorious tree and rock magnets.

Approximate YJ Production
(Calendar Year)
1986: 16,853
1987: 36,114
1988: 52,691
1989: 69,565
1990: 58,184
1991: 65,135
1992: 59,690
1993: 72,901
1994: 70,000
1995: 70,000
1996: 70,000
Total: 632,231

Top: It's tough to see where you're going from this vantage point. What goes up, must come down, and the winch lets the Wrangler down easy.

Inset: If the Tough Truck competition included a front-wheel-drive-only class, this YJ would've been a top contender. However, the grandstand wouldn't necessarily be SRO.

Top: A New York Wrangler takes in some ferny East Coast foliage. Turbine-style wheels are all but extinct now.

Inset: Jeep sports date back to the formation of the earliest clubs. Modified YJs are well suited for obstacle courses and other events that require tight turning.

Popular YJ Exterior Colors
Pearl White
Coffee
Sand Dune Yellow
Metallic Silver
Metallic Spinnaker Blue
Khaki
Vivid Red

Top: In Florida, Wranglers are modified for mud and swamps. Winches are mandatory, and snorkel kits aren't uncommon. Many Ocala-area Jeeps are equipped with onboard air.

Inset: Wranglers are popular with women. Even a modestly modified model such as this Islander edition can access the remote backcountry.

Top: Built by Misch 4x4 Products, this YJ includes TJ-style fatty fender flares, a front Ox Locker, and a winch and driving lights on an aftermarket bumper.

Inset: Flaming mudder for sale, tow-ready. Some cleaning required.

Top: Unlike its coil-conversion XCL kit, Black Diamond's X2 system uses SOA rear leaf springs. The front is a four-link system with coil-over shocks

Inset: Safari Triathlon competitions combined driving maneuvers with timed outdoors events such as canoeing and shooting.

Top: Military axles and long rear coils make this YJ one of the more extreme trail machines that might actually wear a license plate.

Inset: This Texas YJ loses some tools while attempting to conquer Moab's notorious Dump Bump. Many try and few succeed.

This YJ from the Grimm Jeepers club out of Las Vegas carefully descends the Moab slickrock.

"Funny Fender" CJs

"Funny Fender" CJs

To the American masses, the CJ-5 and CJ-7 popularized automotive ruggedness and off-road capability. These 4x4s are largely responsible for imbedding the Jeep mystique in our psyches, birthing the "only in a Jeep" approach to driving.

"Round-fender" Jeeps' roots date back to an experimental-model 1951 CJ-4. This vehicle foreshadowed the civilian CJ-5/military M38A1 (MD platform), including the Hurricane F-head four-cylinder engine and Dana 44 rear axle. The CJ-4's rounded hood made it into production on the CJ-5/M38A1; its fenders split the difference between the thin, angular, previous-generation flat fender, and the MD platform's forward-hanging sheet metal with radiused wheelwells.

The beloved CJ-5 enjoyed one of the longest runs in all of autodom—almost 30 years (1954–1983). Powertrains evolved throughout the 5's maturation, but its chassis underwent only one major revision: AMC put its thumbprint on the vehicle by lengthening the wheelbase 2.5 inches and widening the axles' track widths in 1972.

The longer-wheelbase CJ-6 and CJ-8 (Scrambler) models are often confused. Both had limited productions: the CJ-6 was made from 1955–1981 (export-only from 1977–1981), and the CJ-8 spanned the 1981–1985 model years. Scramblers are identifiable by their longer rear overhangs.

For many enthusiasts, the CJ-7 is the best all-around 4x4 of all time. Its 93.4-inch wheelbase struck a good compromise between occupant comfort and off-road maneuverability. An available factory AMC 304 V-8 on 1972–1981 models (introduced in the 1972 CJ-5) further endeared the CJ-7 to Jeep Universalists who lusted for eight cylinders but had to swap in Ford or Chevy power prior to then.

Upgrades

Aftermarket parts are most plentiful for the 1976–1986 CJs because many of these models are still on and off the road. (Also, AMC threw fewer variables into the mix than Willys and Kaiser.)

Safety should always be first on any Jeep modification list. Rollover protection (i.e., adding a custom cage, if necessary) and quality seatbelts are more than worth the investment even if needed only once.

Brake upgrades also fall into the safety category. Later-model 11-inch drums are an easy retrofit for earlier CJs, and the aftermarket offers a variety of higher-performance front and rear disc conversions. (Factory front discs appeared in 1977; power steering debuted on 1972 models.)

Probably more powertrain combinations have been attempted in CJs than any other vehicle. Ford and GM V-6 and V-8 engine swaps were popular in pre-AMC (1972) CJs, and now many purists like to keep their Universals "all Jeep" by choosing an engine from the AMC V-8 family: 304, 360, 390, or 401. GM V-6 and V-8 swaps remain popular for Jeeps running taller than 33-inch tires, although the EFI engines require aftermarket wiring harnesses; 1996-to-newer V-8 engines can be tricky for CJ owners who must pass emissions testing.

A variety of performance parts are available for the factory six- and eight-cylinder engines. At a minimum, pre-1970s oil bath air cleaners should be swapped to modern paper or cotton-gauze setups to prevent oil spills off-road.

Popular aftermarket power-adders include performance carburetors, retrofitted fuel injection, high-flow intake manifolds, headers, and electronic ignitions. Superchargers are even available for the 4.0L straight-six and the AMC V-8s. Turbochargers aren't widely embraced because of their limited off-idle power gains, and diesel conversions are starting to enjoy cult popularity now that their power outputs offset their weight penalties.

Transmission and T-case swap options are outlined in the literature from aftermarket specialists such as Advance Adapters and Novak Enterprises. Of the OE CJ axles, the early closed-knuckle Dana 25 and 27 front ends are commonly swapped for a later-model (bolt-in) Dana 30 or a custom Dana 44 or 60. This improves component strength, adds a few degrees of steering, and increases traction-differential possibilities.

Along the same lines, any CJ that doesn't have a Dana 44 rear probably should—the AMC Model 20's tubes routinely bend or break at the pumpkin when dealing with greater-than-stock power and/or large tires. Dana 44s that don't live are typically replaced with custom Dana 60s.

Examples of just a few of the infinite CJ customizing possibilities are shown throughout this chapter.

Dive shop owner Brad Grzelka spray-painted his Laredo with Krylon. Superwinch hubs engage the front axle, and a trusty old Warn 8274 gets Grzelka out of trouble.

1981 CJ-7
Owner: Brad Grzelka, Marietta, Georgia
Engine: 1993 Mustang 5.0L V-8
Transmission: Ford T-18, Advance Adapters, Centerforce clutch
Transfer Case: Dana 300
Axles: D44 front, ARB Air Locker; D60 rear, Detroit Locker; 4.56 gears
Suspension: Superlift 4-inch kit, Pro Comp shocks; 3-inch Performance Accessories body lift
Tires: 36x14.50-15 Super Swampers
Wheels: 15x10 Eagle Alloys
Accessories: Warn 8274 winch, Krylon paint, rear ARB bumper, Hella lights

Grzelka's tub was Rhino Lined on the inside. The custom cage doubles as a spare-carrier, and RJS harnesses keep occupants secured to the Steel Horse Super Seats.

The rear bumper is plumbed to store air from the ARB compressor. Overall, this CJ is set up to get there and back.

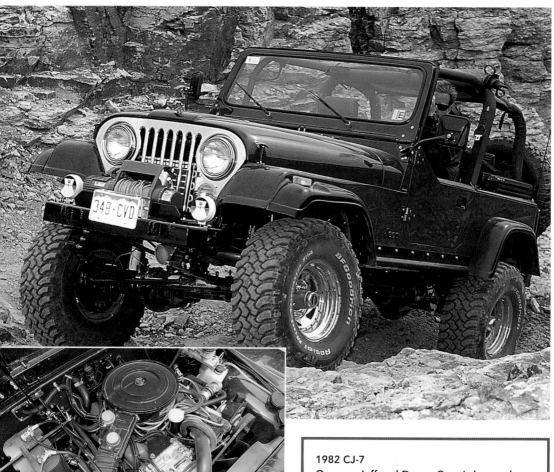

Top: Xenon flares mod the bod over custom burgundy paint; a Warn winch and lights ride on a custom bumper. Lift comes from a spring-over-axle (SOA) conversion.

Inset: Jeff Carr repowered his Jeep with a Howell-injected AMC 360. A York AC compressor supplies onboard air, and a Mepco radiator keeps the 360 from losing its cool.

1982 CJ-7
Owners: Jeff and Donna Carr, Lakewood, Colorado
Engine: AMC 360 V-8, Howell EFI, Flowmaster mufflers
Transmission: TF 727 auto
Transfer Case: Dana 300, Tera Twin Sticks
Axles: D30 front, Detroit Locker; AMC 20 rear, Detroit Locker, Warn shafts; 4.10 gears
Suspension: SOA, Rancho 1-inch springs
Tires: 33x12.50-15 BFG Mud-Terrains
Wheels: 15x8 American Racings
Accessories: Warn HS9500i winch, custom bumpers, Warn lights

Top: A custom swing-away rear carrier was designed to hold a full-sized spare, a big cooler, a jerrican, and a Hi-Lift jack.

Inset: This bird's-eye view reveals Super Seats, a LeCarra steering wheel, a custom cage, Tera T-case Twin Sticks, and remote controls for the Rancho RS9000 shocks.

Top: Tim Taylor's stretched CJ-5 has 17 inches of additional frame behind the front spring hangers. Its spring-over-axle lift uses Superlift leafs, and custom crossover steering combines ground clearance with predictable control.

Inset: Interior upgrades include a diamond-plate floorpan, B&M shifter, six-point roll cage, and Quick Air II compressor with remote air tank.

1980 LWB CJ-5
Owner: Tim Taylor, Nacogdoches, Texas
Engine: Chevy 350 V-8, K&N air cleaner, Hooker headers, Flowmaster mufflers
Transmission: TH400 auto
Transfer Case: Dana 300, TeraLow 4:1 kit and SYE
Axles: D44 front, Detroit Locker; GM 14-bolt rear, Detroit Locker; 4.88 gears
Suspension: Superlift 4-inch SOA, Revolver shackles, Bilstein shocks; 1-inch body lift
Tires: 39.5x18-15 Super Swamper Boggers
Wheels: 15x12 MRT bead locks
Accessories: Warn 8274 winch, KC lights

Top: A Tomken rear bumper/rack and rocker panels handle protection and exterior storage. Revolver shackles provide extra suspension flex.

Inset: The Chevy 350 found a happy home, thanks in part to a custom wiring harness. A Wrangler NW dual battery setup and K&N air cleaner are prominent.

Top: Tuxedo Park trim included nickel-plated bumpers, side mirrors, and hood latches. Nancy Muto's Jeep was spiffed by her husband, who does concours restos on Euro sports cars.

Inset: The interior features a six-point cage, Super Seats, a custom stainless dash, and shock-resistant gauges. A tilt/telescoping column was part of a power-steering conversion.

1970 CJ-5 Tuxedo Park
Owner: Nancy Muto, Danville, California
Engine: Buick 225 V-6
Transmission: T14A three-speed manual, Warn overdrive
Transfer Case: Dana 20
Axles: D27 front, Powr-Lok; D44 rear, Powr-Lok; 5.38 gears
Suspension: Rancho 2.5-inch lift, Edelbrock IAS shocks
Tires: 33x12.50-15 Dunlop Radial Rovers
Wheels: 15x10 American Racings
Accessories: Warn multi-mount 6,000-pound winch, LeCarra steering wheel, stainless panels and knobs

Top: The rear bumper and spare/rack were powder coated. A receiver was added to accommodate the Warn multi-mount winch in the rear.

Inset: Rick Muto rebuilt the factory "Dauntless" Buick V-6, balancing and blueprinting it to put out 160 horsepower and 235 lb-ft of torque on the dyno.

Top: Mike Westphal radiused the rear wheel-wells before spraying on 1991 Camaro Teal Blue paint. Custom rocker armor is also visible.

Inset: A reverse-rotation Dana 60 rear end mini-mizes the rear driveshaft angle. Total lift is 6 inches from Rancho components swapped on top of the axles.

1969 CJ-5
Owner: Mike Westphal, Aurora, Illinois
Engine: Chevy LT-1 V-8, K&N filter, Flex-a-Lite fans
Transmission: SM465 four-speed manual, Blazer bell housing, Centerforce clutch, Advance Adapters chain clutch control
Transfer Case: Dana 300, Advance adapter, Currie Twin-Stick
Axles: D44 front, Detroit Locker; reverse-rotation D60 rear, Detroit Locker; 4.56 gears
Suspension: SOA Rancho 1-inch springs, 1-inch extended shackles
Tires: 36x14.50-15 Radial Super Swampers
Wheels: 15x10 American Racing Outlaw IIs
Accessories: Warn 8274 winch, Postal Jeep (DJ) hood and windshield, custom bumpers and rocker guards

Top: Both bumpers are crafted from 1/4-inch rectangular tubing. The six-point roll cage is also custom.

Inset: Auto Meter gauges are hidden among dash plaques. Westphal has wheeled his CJ from coast to coast, and he has the booty to prove it.

Top: Dr. John Clouse and teenaged son Jacob spent eight years transforming their CJ. They run with the Ozark 4x4 Club.

Inset: Power comes from a Street & Performance Chevy TPI 350. An electric compressor supplies the Air Lockers; an engine-driven Ready Air handles service pneumatics.

1986 CJ-7
Owner: Dr. John Clouse, Springfield, Missouri
Engine: Chevy 350 V-8, dual batteries
Transmission: TH700R4 auto, Hurst shifter
Transfer Case: Dana 300
Axles: D30 front, ARB Air Locker; AMC 20 rear, ARB Air Locker; 4.10 gears
Suspension: Superlift 4-inch kit, Currie shackles
Tires: 33x12.50-15 Goodyear Mud-Terrains
Wheels: 15x10 M/T Alcoas
Accessories: Ramsey winch, custom bumpers, rear-mounted trans cooler, onboard air

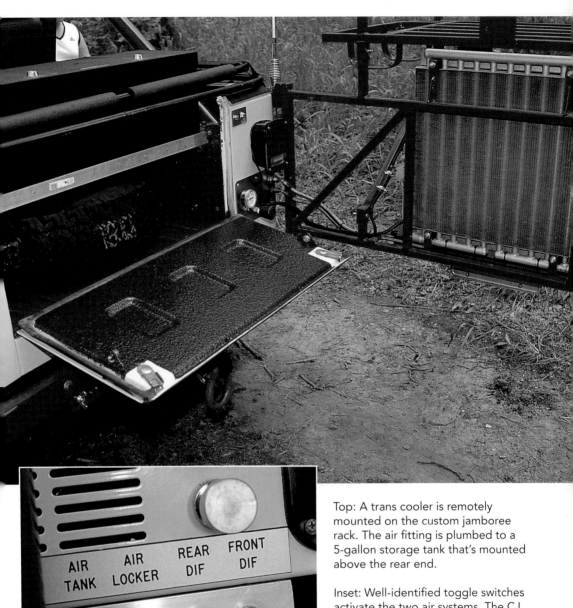

Top: A trans cooler is remotely mounted on the custom jamboree rack. The air fitting is plumbed to a 5-gallon storage tank that's mounted above the rear end.

Inset: Well-identified toggle switches activate the two air systems. The CJ also boasts a 160-amp Wrangler NW alternator, giving it plenty of juice to go with the auxiliary air.

Top: The "Siberian Scrambler" is a heavy-duty freak of a Jeep. It's a CJ-7 in the front, a CJ-8 in the rear, and has a 24-inch stretched frame.

Inset: A Goodwrench crate engine got the nod. Built for business, the powerplant has a Holley Pro-Jection EFI system under the Edelbrock air cleaner.

Hybrid CJ-7/CJ-8
Owners: Kevin and Donna Kaylin, Gaffney, South Carolina
Engine: GM 350 V-8 crate engine, Holley EFI, Weiand intake, Corvette headers
Transmission: TH350 auto, B&M shifter, and shift kit
Transfer Case: NP205
Axles: D60 front, Detroit Locker; GM 14-bolt rear, Detroit Locker; 5.13 gears
Suspension: SOA using stock S-10 leaf packs
Tires: 44-inch Super Swampers
Wheels: 15x12 Eatons
Accessories: Cowl-induction hood, 24-inch stretch

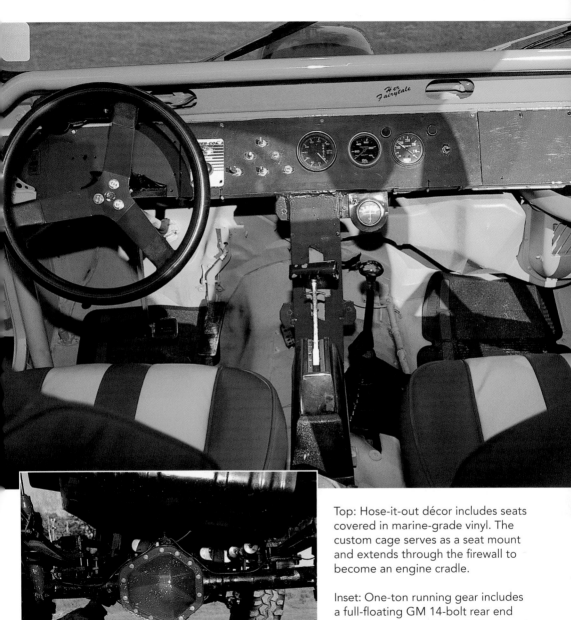

Top: Hose-it-out décor includes seats covered in marine-grade vinyl. The custom cage serves as a seat mount and extends through the firewall to become an engine cradle.

Inset: One-ton running gear includes a full-floating GM 14-bolt rear end with disc brakes, a Dana 60 front end, and an NP205 T-case.

Top: This mechanical marvel is actually more Chevy than Jeep. AMC body parts were widened 10.5 inches and lengthened 6 inches to fit a 1971 Suburban frame.

Inset: Interior highlights include Auto Meter gauges on an aluminum dash panel, a Grant steering wheel, and custom tube work.

1979 CJ-5/Suburban
Owner: Matthew Brusselback, Palm Coast, Florida
Engine: Chevy 454 V-8, Holley 650 double-pumper carb
Transmission: TH400 auto
Transfer Case: NP205
Axles: GM 10-bolt front; GM 14-bolt rear; 3.73 gears
Suspension: Superlift 6-inch front springs; OE GM rear springs w/blocks
Tires: 40-inch Generals
Wheels: 15x14 custom steelies
Accessories: Stretched and widened Jeep body

Xenon 6-inch-wide fender flares create a Scrambler-esque appearance from behind. The 14-inch-wide steel wheels were custom-built.

Axles were scavenged from a 1979 Chevy pickup. Superlift springs lift the front; 4-inch blocks were added to stock Chevy pickup leafs to level the rear.

Top: Making a wake: a CJ-8 traverses a water-crossing, Ramsey winch at the ready. At least the aluminum diamond-plate rockers and corners won't rust.

Inset: It's a drag: the annual Gravelrama event in Cleves, Ohio, attracts Jeeps that are customized for side-by-side sand dragging and hill climbing. Ground clearance and suspension articulation aren't priorities.

CJ Production	
CJ-5:	603,303
CJ-6:	50,172
CJ-7:	379,299
CJ-8:	27,792

Top: Ride the rut: this CJ explores the limits of its leaf-spring suspension articulation. The tire in the air is a minor inconvenience thanks to a locker in the diff.

Inset: Snow and sand are two of the more forgiving nonpavement back-country surfaces. This CJ is cleverly disguised in snow camo.

The short-wheelbase CJ-5 is a maneuverable Tough Truck contender. However, its stubby frame isn't the best at absorbing shock, and this driver likely needed to see a chiropractor as a result of this run.

Some CJ Special Edition Debuts

1961: Tuxedo Park
1962: Tuxedo Park Mark II
1963: Tuxedo Park Mark III
1964: Tuxedo Park Mark IV
1970: Renegade I
1973: Renegade II
1973: Super Jeep
1975: Levi's Package
1978: Golden Eagle
1979: Silver Anniversary
1980: Laredo
1982: Jamboree

A clean CJ-8 named Hector takes a dip in muddy water as a YJ prepares to take the plunge. Note the color coordination between the Jeep's paint and its driver's T-shirt.

Top: Do the dunes: a CJ-7 airs it out at Michigan's Silver Lake ORV area outside of Grand Rapids.

Right: Wyoming-based Rod Pepper sows his Wild Oats on trails throughout the West. The CJ-5 appears frequently in the enthusiast magazines.

Top: Perhaps this CJ-8's owner was still snow-blind when he chose the paint scheme for his Jeep.

Left: This Renegade is still a slave to gravity. Not even hood louvers and an auxiliary air tank could provide the necessary downforce to keep the CJ-7 on all fours.

Next Page: Too fast for fender flares: thrust and inertia can cause broken parts to fly. Mud always seems to stick, though.

Originator leads imitator: in Idaho, a CJ-5 shows an FJ-40 how to behave properly in the snow.

This driver showed incredible forethought by strapping down his hood prior to taking on the Tough Truck course at a Special Events 4x4 Jamboree Nationals event.

Previous Page: These competitors are wearing almost as much dirt as their Jeep. Subtract style points for the Hawaiian-print seat covers clashing with the camo pants, though.

Top: CJ coil conversions are a fad that dates back to the mid-1990s. This setup allows greater axle movement and cushions landings.

Top: This coil-converted CJ hooks onto a rock anchor. We aren't sure where he goes from here.

Inset: A Spud State CJ finds itself in a snowy predicament. The peanut gallery always has all the answers.

Top: Gary Goode is a tool and die maker who bought a CJ-5, then stripped it to the frame. He custom made the front axle by combining a Checker cab rear end with Scout knuckles and remachined shafts.

Inset: Goode sourced a '76 Chevy big block, then fabricated motor mounts and a bell housing adapter to fit it into the CJ.

1974 CJ-5
Owner: Gary Goode, Springboro, Ohio
Engine: GM 454 V-8 crate engine, 750-CFM Carter AFB carb, Edelbrock Performer intake, Hooker headers
Transmission: T-18 four-speed
Transfer Case: Twin-stick Dana 20, PTO
Axles: Custom D60s: 4.10 gears, Powr-Loks
Suspension: Rancho 4-inch suspension lift, Trailmaster shocks; custom 3-inch body lift
Tires: 16/35-15 Super Swamper Boggers
Wheels: 15x14 American Racings
Accessories: Owner-made transmission adapter and rear stainless-steel bumper

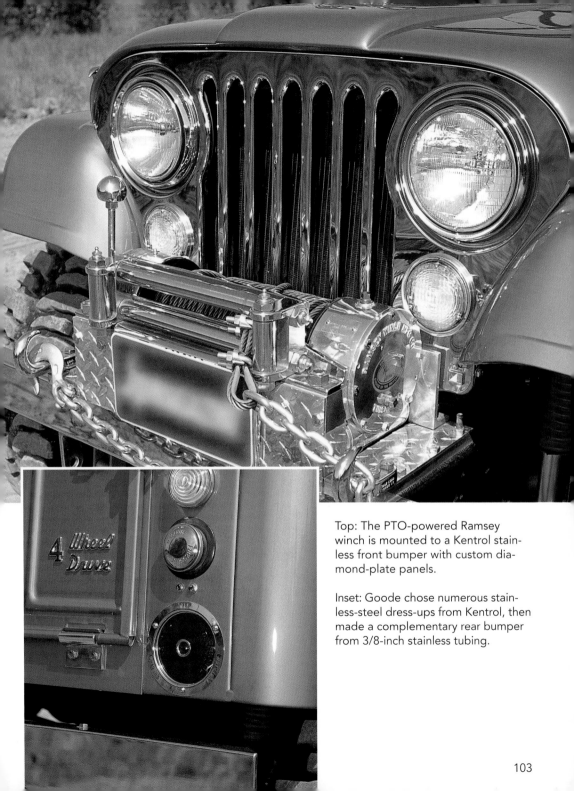

Top: The PTO-powered Ramsey winch is mounted to a Kentrol stainless front bumper with custom diamond-plate panels.

Inset: Goode chose numerous stainless-steel dress-ups from Kentrol, then made a complementary rear bumper from 3/8-inch stainless tubing.

Wagons, Panels, Cherokees, and Wagoneers

Wagons, Panels, Cherokees, and Wagoneers

This chapter isn't titled "Sport Utilities" because, arguably, the early Jeep wagons weren't very sporty. Take-the-family-anywhere utilitarianism seemed to be the initial design priority.

1946–1965
Wagons and Panel Deliveries
Willys-Overland capitalized on its military Jeeps' élan by introducing America's first all-steel (roof and body) wagon—the Model 463—in 1946. With the exception of the "Go-Devil" 134-cubic-inch L-head four-cylinder engine, though, the two-wheel-drive wagon with independent front suspension had little in common with the bobtail military Jeeps and civilian CJ-2A.

An upper-scale 663 model "Station Sedan" debuted in 1948, powered by a 148-cubic-inch "Lightning" six-cylinder engine. Factory four-wheel drive appeared in 1949. Later wagon models—designated for their engines—were the 673 (75-horse-power/161-cubic-inch L-head six), 685 (90-horsepower/161-cubic-inch F-head six), 6-226 (115-horsepower/226-cubic-inch L-head six), and 6-230 (140-horsepower/230-cubic-inch OHC six). Wood-grained body and door panels in the early vehicles and the later two-toned paint schemes helped give the Willys and Kaiser wagons/deliveries a ruggedly attractive look that's proven to be more timeless than their contemporaneous competitors.

1963–1991
Full-sized Wagoneers and Cherokees
Kaiser introduced the J-Series platform in 1963, coinciding with its acquisition of Willys. Wagoneers received the J-100 designation, while pickups were named the J-200 and J-300, depending on wheelbase (changing to J-2000 and J-3000 in 1965).

Notable as the first 4x4 with a factory automatic transmission, the Wagoneer debuted with the OHC 230-cubic-inch six-cylinder engine. This powerplant gave way to the OHV 232-cubic-inch six in 1965; the optional OHV 327-cubic-inch Vigilante V-8. In 1966, the Super Wagoneer began its three-year run. The original luxury utility wagon, the Super Wagoneer came with the Vigilante V-8, and its exorbitant-at-the-time $5,943 MSRP covered upscale amenities such as a power rear window, a vinyl top, and a chromed luggage rack.

The Buick 350 V-8 was introduced for 1968 models, and by 1969 the Wagoneer was available as a four-door 4x4 only. The AMC engine family (258 I-6; 304, 360, 401 V-8s) started appearing in 1972. Quadra-Trac full-time four-wheel drive was available in 1973 models. In 1974, the Cherokee was launched as essentially a less-optioned two-door Wagoneer. Requisite-for-the-era wood-grain paneling characterized Wagoneers starting in 1975, and the Grand Wagoneer survived until 1991 as Jeep's upscale full-sized SUV.

1984–1999
XJ Cherokee/Wagoneer

The XJ compact SUV platform never won any styling awards. However, the vehicle is noteworthy as the first nonmilitary 4x4 with unibody construction. The XJ's durability and off-road capability eventually won over most of its early critics.

The early models were underpowered, offering the stalwart Iron Duke 2.5L four or shoddy GM-built 2.8L V-6. The PowerTech 4.0L inline six, available with the AW-4 automatic, appeared in 1987. In 1991, the High Output version of the 4.0L

was offered along with the durable AX-15 five-speed manual. Much of the rest of the geartrain overlaps the YJ Wrangler.

Suspension is where the XJ shines. Coil-front/leaf-rear Quadra-Link provides a balance between flexibility and stability that caught even Wrangler and CJ owners' attentions as an ideal street-and-trail setup. Lifted, high-articulation XJs are often seen sans doors on the trail to allow the unibody to flex. (The "MJ" Comanche is basically a pickup version of the XJ SUV.)

Overall, the XJ is a significant link in the evolution of the 4x4. It (and possibly the AMC Eagle) foreshadowed the car-based crossover utility-vehicle fad.

1993–2004 ZJ and
WJ Grand Cherokee/Wagoneer

The ZJ was originally conceived as a replacement for the XJ. Instead, it wound up being a snootier sibling to the Cherokee. Although it hasn't been as warmly embraced by Jeep connoisseurs as the other SUVs in the family, the ZJ nonetheless displays impressive off-pavement capabilities with its Quadra Coil suspension. It has a luxurious road ride to boot. In 1999, the WJ Grand upped the ante even further, replacing the ancient Chrysler 318-cubic-inch/5.2L and 360-cubic-inch/5.9L V-8s with the lighter 4.7L PowerTech V-8.

This chapter shows a fraction of the ways enthusiasts have customized Jeep utilities to improve off-road success.

Missouri mudder trucker: 37-inch Boggers flanked by Tomken bumpers, Hella off-road lights, and an ARB Safari snorkel.

1992 Cherokee
Owner: Cory Buermann, Ballwin, Missouri
Engine: 4.0L I-6, Airaid throttle body spacer, Borla header, DynoMax cat-back
Transmission: AX-15
Transfer Case: NP 231, TeraLow 4:1, JB SYE
Axles: Reverse-rotation D44 front, ARB Air Locker; Mark Williams Ford 9-inch rear; 5.13 gears
Suspension: Front Rubicon Express 6-inch coils, Tomken 2-inch spacers, Skyjacker shocks; rear Rubicon Express 4.5-inch springs, 3-inch add-a-leafs, 2.5-inch blocks, Revolver shackles, Rancho shocks
Tires: 37x12.50-15 Super Swamper Boggers
Wheels 15x10 Pro Comp Rock Crawlers
Accessories: Warn 8000i winch, Hella lights

Top: Cory Buermann needed 10 inches of lift for Bogger clearance. Rubicon Express, Tomken, and Sky-jacker suspension parts surround the reverse-rotation D44 pumpkin and crossover steering.

Left: This Cherokee is stocked. The cargo area houses the spare in addition to a 7-gallon air tank, straps, a Hi-Lift jack, and extra axle- and drive-shafts.

Top: Tim Clark's family wagon has adventured to Colorado, Moab, Tellico, Kentucky, and Indy. That's a Warn winch atop an Olympic bumper.

Inset: The well-detailed engine house is highlighted by Clark's custom intake tube that backs a K&N filter.

1991 Cherokee
Owner: Tim Clark, Farmersville, Ohio
Engine: 4.0L I-6, K&N air cleaner, Borla exhaust
Transmission: AX-15
Transfer Case: Atlas II
Axles: D30 front, ARB Air Locker; D44 rear, ARB Air Locker, Grand Cherokee discs; 4.10 gears
Suspension: Front Rubicon Express ZJ 4.5-inch coils, TeraFlex control arms, Off Road General Store trac bar; rear Rusty's 6.5-inch springs and shackles; Pro Comp shocks
Tires: 33x12.50-15 BFG MT/KM
Wheels: 15x8.5 Center Line Convo-Pro
Accessories: Warn XD9000i winch, Olympic front bumper, aluminum roof rack, custom nerf bars, and rear bumper

A 4-foot by 5-foot roof rack was fabbed from aluminum to keep the XJ from getting too top-heavy. It houses the full-sized spare, extinguisher, and overflow road-trip gear.

Components from Kilby Enterprises converted a second AC compressor into an engine-driven onboard air system.

1983 Cherokee Chief
Owner: Kaylene Woo, Gainesville, Florida
Engine: AMC 360 V-8, Edelbrock 750-CFM carb, Edelbrock Performer intake, Hedman headers
Transmission: TF 727 auto, B&M SuperCooler
Transfer Case: NP208
Axles: D44 front, ARB Air Locker; AMC 20 rear, Detroit SofLocker; 3.73 gears
Suspension: Rusty's 4-inch lift, Rancho shocks, Rubicon Express sway bar disconnects, 2-inch Performance Accessories body lift
Tires: 35x12.50-15 Goodyear MT/Rs
Wheels: 15x10 Eagle Outlaw IIs
Accessories: True Radius brush guard, Warn 10,000-pound winch, KC & PIAA lights

Top: Kaylene Woo makes quite a splash in her Chief, even on the pavement. She's the unofficial Chieftan of Gainesville, Florida.

Inset: The OE AMC 360 was rebuilt and Edelbrocked to put out 300 horsepower/360 lb-ft on the dyno. Dress-ups include the logo'd air cleaner, stainless overbraided plumbing, and red plug wires.

The front is enhanced by True Radius armor, KC lights, and a Warn 10,000-pound winch. A Rusty's 4-inch lift makes way for the 35-inch MT/Rs.

Herculiner roll-on bedliner coats in the interior sheet metal, and Dynamat sound-absorption material improves cocoon comfort.

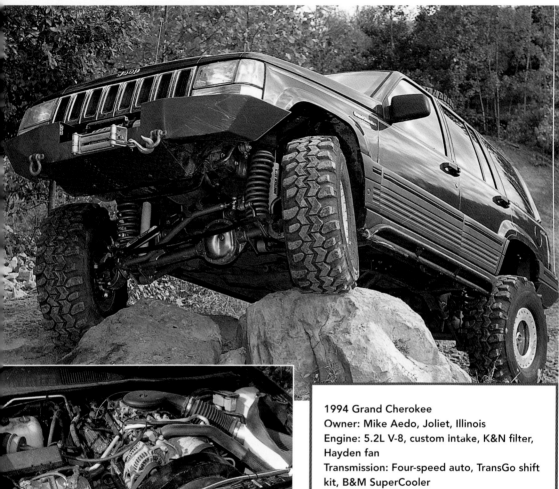

Top: Mike Aedo picked up his ZJ as a $4,000 repo. A bit of bumper and fender trimming allow the Grand to flex without rubbing.

Inset: Underhood air management was upgraded. An owner-fabbed intake uses a K&N filter, and cooling was upgraded with a Hayden fan clutch and big-block blades.

1994 Grand Cherokee
Owner: Mike Aedo, Joliet, Illinois
Engine: 5.2L V-8, custom intake, K&N filter, Hayden fan
Transmission: Four-speed auto, TransGo shift kit, B&M SuperCooler
Transfer Case: NP242, 4:1 kit
Axles: D30 front; D35 rear, LockRite; 4.10 gears, Warn shafts and hubs
Suspension: Rubicon Express 4.5-inch lift, Doetsch Tech shocks, Rubicon Express sway bar disconnects; 2-inch Performance Accessories body lift
Tires: 33-inch Super Swampers
Wheels: 15x8 Champion bead locks
Accessories: Ramsey REP 8000-pound winch, custom rock sliders

Both axles have hardened Warn shafts and hubs. Aedo fabbed his own rock sliders.

The Dana 35 was built with a Warn full-floater kit and disc brakes: CJ-7 rotors and Chevy S-10 calipers. Rubicon Express springs provide the lift.

Top: Willys engineers likely didn't envision the wagon in Canary Yellow and Magenta. The body style is more timeless than most other post-war wagons.

Right: The color scheme extends to the undercarriage. Superlift springs and shocks are surrounded by yellow U-bolts, driveshafts, backing plate, crossmember, and steering linkage.

1946 Model 463 Wagon Specifications	
Wheelbase:	104.0 inches
Length:	176.3 inches
Height:	72.8 inches
Width:	68.8 inches
Curb Weight:	2,935 pounds

Left: The front end looks like it could use some caster shims to lessen the operating angle of the front driveshaft's U-joints.

Bottom: Crossed Up Off Road's 1998 Cherokee has evolved into a competition "Truggy" since this photo was taken at Moab's Potato Salad Hill. It features Ford 9-inch axles and a custom suspension.

SJ Full-Size Wagoneer Specifications

Wheelbase: 110.0 inches
Length: 183.7 inches
Height: 64.2 inches
Width: 75.6 inches
Curb Weight: 3,700 pounds

Below: Hardcore Cherokee owners routinely leave their doors behind before things get flexy. Cigarette butts are highly optional and require additional driving skill.

Previous: Fording Jeep: an ARB bull bar leads this XJ down a water crossing. Its Skyjacker lift kit and Mickey Thompson rubber get the undercarriage up above the rocks.

Below: This Cherokee is mildly massaged with headlight rock guards and a Con-Ferr (now Off-Road Unlimited Defender) roof rack.

Previous: "The road to paradise is not paved" according to the Grimm Jeepers of Las Vegas.

Top: For this Lone Star XJ, mud—not oil—
might be the real Texas tea.

Bottom: A stream in the Four Corners area
poses no problem for this Cherokee. Secure
front license-plate mounting locations are
sparse on winch-equipped XJs.

XJ Specifications	
Wheelbase:	101.4 inches
Length:	165.3 inches
Height:	63.3 inches
Width:	70.5 inches
Curb Weight:	3,600 pounds

All stickered up and going nowhere—at least until a few friends jump on board to help tires contact rocks.

Tall aftermarket coil springs provide XJs with an impressive amount of suspension travel and flexibility.

XJs take to snow like Canadians to ice hockey. This Sport model is built with a Rubicon Express suspension and aftermarket bumpers.

ZJ Specifications	
Wheelbase:	105.9 inches
Length:	179.0 inches
Height:	64.8 inches
Width:	70.9 inches
Curb Weight:	3,530 pounds

XJ Wagoneers were made from 1984–1990. Four headlights sometimes distinguished them from the Cherokee version. Wagoneer Limiteds got the classic woodgrain side graphics.

Blasphemy? Note the Warn winch on an XJ that's competing in the Ramsey National Off-Road Challenge. Nerf bars appear worse for wear.

The North American XJ Association is a vital resource for Cherokee owners. This "Rusty'd" XJ was photographed at an association event in Tellico, Tennessee.

Top: Full-sized spare tires create a dilemma for XJ owners. Inside, they occupy much of the cargo area. This family needs space for the baby seat and diaper bag.

Right: ZJ Grands typically don't play as dirty as XJs. However, second and third owners seem less hesitant to modify them for severe trail duty.

WJ Specifications	
Wheelbase:	105.9 inches
Length:	181.5 inches
Height:	69.4 inches
Width:	72.3 inches
Curb Weight:	3,669 pounds

This ZJ's owner apparently drew the short straw and got trail-breaking duties. Either that or he was goofing off and got in a little over his head.

Like most Jeeps, showroom-stock Grands can get to many scenic backcountry areas, such as this stretch of the San Juan range in southwest Colorado.

Although the WJ Grand looks similar to its predecessor, the two vehicles reportedly only share 127 parts, mostly nuts and bolts.

This ZJ is set up for Sno-Blind success with an ARB front bumper and Warn winch.

Wagoneer Model-Year Production	
1974:	13,746
1975:	16,708
1976:	21,912
1977:	20,298
1978:	28,871
1979:	27,437
1980:	10,481
1981:	13,741
1982:	18,709
1983:	18,478
1984:	20,019
1985:	17,814
1986:	17,254
1987:	14,265
1988:	14,117
1989:	10,159
1990:	6,449
1991:	1,560
1992:	330

DaimlerChrysler thrashes even the most expensive members of the Jeep family to ensure their off-road capability is worthy of the nameplate.

Compete in a late-model luxury SUV? Only in North America (and possibly the Middle East?).

This WJ reposes high above timberline near the abandoned mines outside of Telluride, Colorado. These views are only accessible by foot, beast of burden, dirt bike, or four-wheel drive.

Joel Snider's Stage West 1998 ZJ is a daily driver. It has a 3-inch lift, 32-inch Goodyear ATs, custom 2x2-inch rocker guards, and an ARB front bumper with a Warn winch.

Cherokee Model-Year Production	
1974:	14,082
1975:	16,294
1976:	26,365
1977:	33,684
1978:	40,698
1979:	39,183
1980:	7,614
1981:	6,321
1982:	6,911
1983:	6,186

Super Swamper Boggers add to the Willys' already-aggressive attitude. V-grille models look particularly menacing.

Cherokees are virtually synonymous with snow country. Just add snow tires and go.

Jeepsters, FCs, and FSJ Pickups

Jeepsters, FCs, and FSJ Pickups

This chapter is the catch-all for notable but less popular Jeep models. Because off-road performance is the gist of this book, we're purposely ignoring the two-wheel-drive DJ-model Dispatch and Postal Jeeps. Some of the other more obscure Jeeps, such as the FCs, aren't represented pictorially simply because they aren't prevalent at off-road events.

Pickups

Built on the Wagon platform, a Willys pickup was introduced in 1947. It was offered in both 4x2 and 4x4 versions, the latter in a one-ton cargo rating. Factory bed options included utility bodies, stakebeds, flatbeds, and even a tow-truck configuration. The truck was redesigned in 1950, receiving a V-shaped grille and 473 model designation. This was also the final year for two-wheel-drive versions.

In 1953, the designation changed to 475, following suit with the wagons and deliveries. The six-cylinder 6-226 model appeared in 1954 and was replaced by the 6-230 (powered by the Tornado OHC I-6) in 1962.

Jeep's pickup line became Gladiators in 1963, built on the same platform as the Wagoneer. J200 signified short wheelbase and J300 designated long wheelbase until 1965, replaced by J2000, J3000, and J4000 (131-inch wheelbase). Bed variations were standard Townside, stepside Thriftside, and stakebed. The Gladiator name was dropped after 1971, simplified with J2000 and J4000 through 1973, and the J10 and J20 from 1974 to 1988. Regional "Mucho Macho" Honcho sporty trim debuted in 1977. It included special wheels, side graphics, and, in later years, a bed bar and brushguard. These full-sized Jeeps (FSJs) have survived the tests of time and recently enjoyed a surge in popularity. (Jeep's 1985–1992 mini-truck experiment—the Comanche—was basically an XJ Cherokee with a bed instead of a second-row seat and enclosed cargo area.)

Jeepsters

Willys designed its VJ-designated Jeepster as an attempt to crash the sports car market in 1948 with a Jeep-branded vehicle. Buyers weren't overly receptive to the rear-wheel-drive car, although the automotive press praised the vehicle. A three-year run ended in the 1950 model year; 19,132 VJs were sold.

The Jeepster name was revived in 1966, attached to the C101-platform Commando. Sharing powertrains with the CJ-5 but featuring a 101-inch wheelbase, the Commando combined the CJ's off-road attitude in a package that wasn't as clunky as the full-sized wagons.

AMC dropped the Jeepster prefix in 1971 and redesigned the Commando for 1972, designating it the C104 (again, for the wheelbase). The three available engines were the Buick-designed 225-cubic-inch V-6, the AMC 258-cubic-inch I-6, and the AMC 304-cubic-inch V-8. Unfortunately, the Commando disappeared after 1973, presumably to clear the way for the CJ-7.

Forward Controls

Probably the quirkiest Jeeps were the Forward Control models, produced from 1956 to 1965. Cab-over-engine styling foreshadowed the infamous VW Microbus.

The two available models were the 81-inch-wheelbase FC-150 and 108-inch-wheelbase FC-170. Most FCs were used for industry, outfitted as tow trucks, fire trucks, for forestry service, and myriad other duties; an FC-170 dually was even produced. As such, FCs are rare sights at recreational four-wheeling events, popping up more often at tea-party-on-the-lawn-type automotive gatherings.

Top: This High Country Commando conquers the Rockies with a Ramsey winch. More subtle modifications include diamond-plate rocker protectors and off-road lights.

Bottom: Subaru seats increase the comfort coefficient. Other interior adornments include white-faced Auto Meter gauges and a Tuffy console.

1970 Jeepster Commando
Owners: Eric Pape and Kat Gilmartin, Bailey, Colorado
Engine: Chevy 350 V-8, QuadraJet
Transmission: Clark close-ratio five-speed manual
Transfer Case: Dana 300, Currie Twin-Stick
Axles: D44 front, ARB Air Locker; D44 rear, Detroit TrueTrac; 4.56 gears
Suspension: OME springs, Revolver shackles, dual Black Diamond shocks
Tires: 33x12.50-15 Yokohama Geolanders
Wheels: 15x8 Pumas
Accessories: Ramsey REP 8000 winch, custom bumpers

Old Man Emu CJ springs and extended shackles raise the front a total of four inches. Power steering was sourced from a 1992 TJ.

A custom spare carrier and can holder attends to business in the rear. The Kayline ragtop provides removable weather protection.

Top: Andrew Langefels spent five years resurrecting a seldom-seen J10 Stepside. He let his fingers do the mousing to find replacement parts.

Bottom: FSJs are riding a wave of popularity. They're rugged and easier on the eyes to most than the I-H trucks of their eras.

1981 J10 Stepside
Owner: Andrew Langefels, Durango, Colorado
Engine: AMC 360 V-8, Comp cam, Holley EFI
Transmission: T176 four-speed manual
Transfer Case: Dana 300
Axles: D44 front; AMC 20 rear, limited-slip; 3.31 gears
Suspension: Trailmaster 4-inch lift, Black Diamond shocks
Tires: 33x12.50-15 BFG All-Terrains
Wheels: 15x10 American Racings
Accessories: Frenched taillights

Langefels recessed the taillights into the fenders for a cleaner look. The bed bar gives it a classic 1980's *CHiPs* personality (although the J10 lacks KC lights).

The stock 360 was totally rebuilt: bored .040 over and assembled with a Comp cam, Accel ignition, Holley Pro-Jection, and K&N air cleaner.

Steve Johnston created a resto-mod Commando in part by welding CJ-5 front fenders to the OE cowl and fabricating his own rockers/flares.

The half-cab top wasn't an overly popular factory option, making this clean Commando somewhat rare. Stock bumpers retain the factory élan.

1969 Jeepster Commando Half-Cab
Owner: Steve Johnston, Greencastle, Indiana
Engine: Stock Buick 225 c.i. V-6, custom dual exhaust
Transmission: T-14A manual
Transfer Case: Dana 20
Axles: D27 front; D44 rear; 3.73 gears
Suspension: Rancho SOA, 8-inch lift
Tires: 36x12.50-15 Buckshot Radial Mudders
Wheels: 15x8 American Racing Optimas
Accessories: Custom fenders, rocker panels, paint by J.C. Paint & Body

Keeping the stock oil bath air cleaner and Rochester one-barrel carb pay tribute to the Jeep's origins. A power-steering conversion transplants later-model technology.

The entire tub was sprayed Porsche Red inside and out. Spray-on bedliner material inside helps fend off rust.

This J10 would be truly amazing if the cow theme on its lid were extended over the tonneau cover and the rest of the sheet metal.

1947–1965 Pickup Specifications	
Wheelbase:	118.0 inches
Length:	183.8 inches
Height:	74.4 inches
Width:	73.0 inches
Curb Weight:	3,100 pounds

Top: The Comanche (MJ platform designation) was a pickup version of the XJ Cherokee. Although not overly popular, some were outfitted for desert racing in the southwestern United States.

Bottom: Although this sand-dragger likely has few original Jeep parts, the Jeepster Commando body lines seem to go well with the rear paddle tires.

The Gladiator is one of the rare vehicles that actually lives up to its name. This Buckeye-built example is virtually unstoppable.

Commando Specifications	
Wheelbases:	101, 104 inches
Lengths:	168, 175 inches
Height:	64.1 inches
Width:	65.2 inches
Curb Weight:	3,000 pounds

Commandos seem to have a perfect wheelbase for Tough Truck success: long enough to absorb some bumps but short enough for nimbleness.

Military Jeeps
and Flat-Fenders

Military Jeeps and Flat-Fenders

The Jeep legend came from its grace under fire. As the late Granville King wrote about the year 1942 in his *Jeep Bible*, "Allied victories [happened] everywhere that Jeeps're shipped. Odd coincidence."

In general, flat-fender Jeeps that remain in decent shape are worth more restored or "resto-modded" with minor modernizations such as 12-volt electrics and paper-element air cleaners. The military Jeeps used in *M*A*S*H* reportedly sold for astronomical sums after the show wrapped. The scenario is different for basket-case flat-fenders: imagination and budget are the only resurrection limitations.

1942–1945 Willys MB

The one that won the war: Its 60-horsepower/105 lb-ft 134.2-cubic-inch four-cylinder engine sealed the deal for Willys. Head engineer Barney Roos (who was also president of the Society of Automotive Engineers at the time) convinced the government that its 1,300-pound benchmark vehicle was highly unrealistic; the MB's curb weight came in at 2,315 pounds. The first 25,808 vehicles had welded slat grilles and the Willys name in the rear panel. The signature Jeep multi-bar stamped-steel grille appeared later in 1942 models (8 bars for WWII models, 6 bars for others), and the Willys rear embossing disappeared.

1942–1945 Ford GPW

The government contracted Ford to build military Jeeps to Willys specs. The common misconception is that GPW stands for General Purpose Willys. The G actually indicated that the vehicle was contracted by the government, P was code for 80-inch-wheelbase reconnaissance vehicle, and W stood for the Willys design. Visual differences between the GPW and MB were subtle. Ford stamped its "F" script on many parts, and some early-run vehicles had the Ford logo stamped into their tubs' rear panels.

1944–1945 CJ-2

Willys decided to capitalize on the Jeep's well-known wartime accomplishments with a civilian version, the famous CJ (Civilian Jeep). No documentation exists on a CJ-1, but a dozen "Agri-jeeps" bearing CJ-2 serial numbers were built in 1944. The following year, either 22 or 23 CJ-2s were manufactured. Few still exist, making the CJ-2 one of the most collectible of all Jeeps—certainly of the nonmilitary models.

1945–1949 CJ-2A

The 2A was Willys' first mass-produced Civilian Jeep (CJ). Many MB components carried over, the notable exceptions being larger-diameter headlights (seven inches instead of six), the spare tire mounted on the passenger's side instead of the rear, a tailgate, "Willys" block letters stamped into the windshield frame and sides of the hood, power windshield wipers, and a gas filler tube that extended through the body. Mechanically, the CJ had softer springs, lighter-valved shocks and the T-90 three-speed manual transmission instead of the military's T-84, and a Dana 41 rear axle.

1949–1953 CJ-3A

This was the first CJ with a one-piece windshield. It received an upgraded Dana-Spicer 44 rear axle to replace the previous model 41.

1950–1952 M-38

Built on the same MC-code platform as the CJ-3A, this military version had a beefier frame, stiffer suspension, headlight guards, blackout lights, and 24-volt electrics.

1953–1968 CJ-3B

The "high hood" was created to clear the new "Hurricane" F-head engine. Many 3Bs were exported, and others were built in India as Mahindras.

1967–1969 Kaiser M715

The M715 is the military version of the Jeep Gladiator pickup. With a 2,500-pound cargo capacity, this 1-1/4-ton vehicle is often referred to as a "five-quarter"-ton truck. The stoutest Jeep ever, approximately 30,500 M715s were built during an abbreviated production run. The truck was powered by the 230-cubic-inch Tornado OHC inline-six, backed by a T98A manual transmission and a divorced NP200 transfer case. Top speed in stock form is approximately 60 miles per hour. Its siblings are the M724 cab/chassis, M725 ambulance, and M726 service truck.

This chapter barely scratches the surface of military Jeeps and other related vehicles. Military-vehicle enthusiasts are encouraged to investigate the scores of other books and websites devoted to combat vehicles.

Top: Dana Butters stayed fairly true to his MB's 1943 offerings, making a few changes to create a driver instead of a museum piece.

Bottom: The L-head engine was balanced and blueprinted during a rebuild. Butters converted to 12-volt electrics, a Delco alternator, and a CJ-2A air cleaner.

1943 MB
Owner: Dana Butters, Apple Valley, California
Engine: L-134 flathead I-4
Transmission: T-90 three-speed manual
Transfer Case: Dana 18
Axles: D25 front, Powr-Lok; D41 rear; 4.88 gears
Suspension: Stock
Tires: 6.50-15 Power Kings
Wheels: 15x8 stock steel
Accessories: Military-issue tools

Butters kept the original-style tools intact. To true Jeep enthusiasts, olive drab is the American equivalent of British Racing Green.

Cockpit improvements include Auto Meter gauges, a roll cage, and vinyl upholstery. Sharp eyes will recognize the T-90 shift boot, an update over the stock T-84 three-speed.

Top: Trucks don't get much more serious than the Kaiser M715. Add big Bogger tires and olive drab becomes quite menacing.

Right: The stock Tornado six-cylinder engine didn't live up to its name performance-wise. Reliability was another issue, and V-8 swaps are common for these heavy trucks.

The jerrican and axe pay tribute to the M715's military heritage. The suspension lift gives the M715 greater ground clearance and an utterly aggressive attitude.

This well-preserved M715 still has its original info. Military specs apparently required service, maintenance, and driving requirements to be spelled out.

As Mazarek's license plate proclaims, the foundation of the vehicle is all Jeep. He personalized the flat-fender with an array of aftermarket accessories.

Mark Mazarek inherited the 1946 flattie from its original owner, his grandfather. Instead of updating the 1940s mechanicals, he chose to shorten a CJ-5's chassis two inches and retain the 1970s technology.

1946 CJ-2A/1978 CJ-5
Owner: Mark Mazarek, Warren, Ohio
Engine: AMC 304 V-8, Edelbrock 600-CFM carb, Hedman headers
Transmission: T-150 three-speed manual
Transfer Case: Dana 20
Axles: D30 front, AMC 20 rear; 3.54 gears
Suspension: Black Diamond add-a-leafs and shocks, 3-inch body lift
Tires: 33x12.50-15 Super Swampers
Wheels: 15x10 American Racings
Accessories: Stainless Kentrol bumpers, nerf bars

Black Diamond add-a-leafs and longer shocks combine with a 3-inch body lift to create clearance for 33-inch tires. The powertrain is an aftermarket-massaged 1978 AMC issue.

More-modern body additions include Bushwacker fender flares, Kentrol nerfs and bumpers, and DuPont Medium Green base/clear paint.

Here's a fine example of a mildly resto-modded CJ-3A. The Ramsey winch and Bushwacker fender flares are two purely functional add-ons.

Plenty of replacement parts—many of which are better than the originals—are still available for 3As. These include vinyl (not canvas) tops and soft doors.

Buick V-6s are popular repowering options when the stock "Go Devil" gives up the ghost. The Buick 225-c.i. version was offered in CJ-5s.

Seats and a center console are some of the only concessions here to more-modern amenities and creature comforts.

Top: Some flat-fenders are simply classic bodies atop a fully custom 4x4. Fiberglass and repro metal flattie tubs are available from the aftermarket.

Left: Although the gauge layout has somewhat of a 1940s feel, the rest of the cockpit is competition-ready to today's standards.

This CJ-3A likely mutated from a leaf-sprung Jeep into this long-travel, quad-coiled mechanical marvel.

Corvette engines are some of the best power-to-weight options for Jeep swaps. Late-model TPI fueling is reliable on uneven terrain.

Top: From this angle, the CJ-3B almost looks like a CJ-5, particularly with the diamond-plate rear corners and rocker reinforcers.

Bottom: Flat fenders are particularly space-challenged. Jamboree racks are popular with the trail crowd, and back seats are fairly rare due to the premium on cargo space.

U.S. Flat-Fender Production	
1941 MA	1,553
1942–1945 MB	361,339
1942–1945 Ford GPW	277,896
1944–1945 CJ-2	34 (including Agrijeeps)
1945–1949 CJ-2A	214,202
1949–1953 CJ-3A	131,843
1950–1952 M-38	61,423
1951 CJ-4	1
1953–1968 CJ-3B	155,494

This appears to be a phantom flat fender. The rounded hood and Jeep stamping in front of the door blow its cover as a CJ-5, but the custom front fenders and folded-down windshield make it enough of a wannabe flattie to fit in this chapter.

The Jeep was designed for combat in a variety of conditions, including snow. Mother Nature seems to have a leg up on what looks like a CJ-3A. A proven-over-the-generations Warn 8274 winch stands at the ready.

The windshield looks like CJ-3B issue, but the low hood says CJ-3A. Regardless of what its title says, this custom Willys features front coil-over shocks and Super Swampers on bead lock wheels.

Many Jeep purists find the high-hood CJ-3B disproportionate. The extra hood clearance eases V-8 swaps, which this example likely has.

M715s are the quintessential war wagons. As the stoutest Jeep ever built, they're well-suited to tough-truck-type competitions.

Previous Page: The M-38 is the military version of the CJ-3A. Its stiffer frame doesn't flex as well as the civilian model but holds up better over the decades.

Top: Although the American version of the CJ-3B trickled off the Toledo assembly line for 15 years, the high-hood design is more prevalent overseas: Many 3Bs were exported, and Jeep licensed the vehicle to be produced in India under the Mahindra brand.

Bottom: Rust is a prime reason why few flat-fenders survive today in pristine condition. This CJ-3B owner apparently enjoys the extra clearance and cooling benefits offered by rotting sheet metal.

M715 Specifications	
Wheelbase, inches:	126
Length, inches:	209
Height, inches:	95
Width, inches:	85
Curb Weight, pounds:	5,500

For some reason, M715s seem to attract mud. The custom spare carrier appears inspired by desert racers instead of mud runners.

Once the decision is made to stretch a CJ-3A, why not go all out and hack the hood to make way for a blown big block?

Flat fenders continue to take people to out-of-the-way places—just like they have since 1942.

The military-mandated 80-inch wheelbase makes the flat-fender well suited to rock-crawling competitions.

Is that Bo or Luke behind the wheel of General Willy E. Lee? We assume that the rear-seat passenger answers to Daisy.

The M715 is actually a forefather of the military Hummer. Dimensions are similar, but most Jeep enthusiasts would pick the Kaiser pickup over the overpriced AM General 4x4 any day.

Jeeping Into the Future

Jeeping Into the Future

The Jeep Universal set the standard for off-road capability. Not long after the Willys MB was introduced, the imitators began crawling out from behind rocks: Land Rover Series I, Toyota Land Cruiser, Nissan Patrol, and, later, the Suzuki SJ40/Samurai. Jeep engineers were undoubtedly flattered. Although each of these knock-offs has its advantages (e.g., rust-resistant aluminum bodies for the Rover, stout frame and axles for the Land Cruiser), piloting one just isn't the same as being in the real deal. The copycats have a generic feel; driving a genuine Jeep makes you feel connected to world history.

In the twenty-first century, Jeep's challenge is adapting to a world that has more pavement every day without losing the off-road legacy that's the brand's foundation. The company's Trail Rated standard attempts to maintain Jeep's four-wheel-drive heritage. To qualify for the Trail Rated badge, current 4x4 models must meet minimum off-road performance standards for maneuverability, suspension articulation, traction, ground clearance, and water fording.

Liberty

Introduced for the 2002 model year, the KJ-designation Liberty replaced the beloved Cherokee (although the KJ wears the Cherokee name outside of North America). Introduced to compete with the Ford Escape in the compact SUV segment, the Liberty's historical claim to fame—aside from being the Cherokee killer—is its reintroduction of the diesel engine to the United States in an under-3/4-ton 4x4. Although the Italian-made 2.8L VM Motori engine is somewhat underwhelming, it provides a glimpse into the future of 4x4 power.

WK Grand Cherokee

This next-generation Grand was launched for 2005. Visually similar to its WJ predecessor, the WK is the epitome of Jeep refinement. Although the independent front suspension is a concession to the pavement-pounding suburban professional, this Grand still has decent off-road prowess underneath all its amenities. The available-for-2007 Mercedes-built 3.0L common-rail diesel engine improves the WK's off-road torque without drawing attention to the fact that it's an oil-burning powerplant.

XK Commander

Built on the same platform as the WK Grand Cherokee but with a fatter body, the Commander debuted for the 2006 model year. This true seven-passenger Jeep has the hipper-than-Suburban-owning soccer mom in its cross hairs. Still, the Commander has earned its Trail Rated stripes.

JK Wrangler

New for 2007 was the JK Wrangler. This vehicle will undoubtedly continue Jeep's legendary mastery of unpaved rights of way—particularly once the JK's "place-holder" minivan engine is replaced by a Hemi or diesel. Details aside, the Jeep has come full circle, complete with irony: from making its name in a European-based war to its future being determined by a German parent company.

Introduced as a 2007 model, the JK Wrangler is already an aftermarket favorite. Its main shortcoming is an unspectacular 3.8L V-6. Customizers are already swapping in Hemi V-8 engines, and the JK will undoubtedly get a more worthy powerplant from the factory in the near future.

The Liberty was perhaps Jeep's first unapologetic foray into the pavement-predominate market. Few purists consider it a "real" Jeep.

Liberty Specifications	
Wheelbase, inches:	104.2
Length, inches:	174.7
Height, inches:	71.8
Width, inches:	71.8
Curb Weight, pounds:	4,033

The 4x4 Liberty is Trail Rated by Jeep to meet certain off-road standards. Already a cult vehicle, the KJ has a few owners' groups.

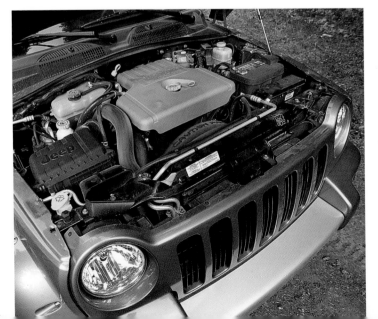

Liberty's main claim to fame is its available diesel engine. Although the Italian-built VM 2.8L CRD (common-rail diesel) is unrefined by modern American pickup standards, it foreshadows engines of the future.

Unveiled for 2005, the WK Grand Cherokee seems almost too luxurious for a Jeep. Apparently you can have it all.

WK Grand Cherokee Specifications	
Wheelbase, inches:	109.5
Length, inches:	186.7
Height, inches:	67.4
Width, inches:	82.4
Curb Weight, pounds:	4,490

The Grand's Quadra-Drive II four-wheel-drive system takes some of the decisions away from the driver. For the average buyer, this is a good thing.

Top: Built on the same platform as the WK Grand Cherokee, the Commander is two inches longer and has a larger body to accommodate seven passengers comfortably.

Bottom: The Commander is somewhat of a throwback vehicle, calling to mind the chunky greatness of the Grand Wagoneer. Maybe fake woodgrain side panels will be optional at some point.

Commander Specifications	
Wheelbase, inches:	109.5
Length, inches:	188.5
Height, inches:	71.9
Width, inches:	89.0
Curb Weight, pounds:	5,091